The Soul's Openner

Also by Torry Fountinhead

The 7 Pillars Your Authentic Self Stands On, Part I of The Essential Companion Series

The Beauty, Part of The Contemplation Series

The Lake That Hides The Dummy, Part of The Rainbow of Life's Secrets

Poem: Good Enough, Part of Forever Spoken, The International Library of Poetry

and many more at work...

The Soul's Openner

Enchanting the Soul to 'Being'

Part II of "Contemplations" Series

By **Torry Fountinhead**

Airé Libré Publishing & Computing Ltd.

1st Printing & Publishing April 25th 2011

The cover illustration, drawn by Torry Fountinhead, on January 16th 2002, to represent the culminating expression of a Human-Being.

©2004 Torry Meirah Fountinhead

ISBN-10: 0-9733450-8-X

ISBN-13: 978-0-9733450-8-7

All Rights of this work are Reserved. No part or whole may be used, copied or reproduced, stored in retrieval systems, or transmitted, in any form or by any means whatsoever, including electronic media, mechanical, photocopying, recording, or otherwise. For more information contact:
Airé Libré Publishing & Computing Ltd.
Suite 306, 185-911 Yates St.
Victoria BC V8V 4Y9 Canada
Tel: 1-250-592-3099.
Http://www.al.bc.ca info@al.bc.ca

Book Web-Site URLs:
Http://www.thesoulsopenner.com
Http://www.truthresonancegong.com
Http://www.divinespark.ca

Like a spirit floating over the water
I felt today looking at the blue sea
Gentle waves moved by the gentle breeze
Me and the sail boats colouring the wind

Table of Contents

The Soul's Openner—3
A Bundle of Tales—1
Spiritual Place of Seclusion—5
The Ultimate Sublime & The Truth-Resonance-Gong—9
Assimilation of Realization—13
Belief Systems & Our Soul—19
Finding & Redefining —25
Understanding Your Value—33
What Is Our Work?—39
Faith—43
The Beauty—47
Hope—51
The Path Joy versus Hardship—55
Aids to the Unveiling—61
At The Gate—73
The Openner—77
Your Soul Is Shining—83
Maintaining The Openness—87

Ponder This:

"If you believe your destination,

        you become your goal."

                           TF 2004

The Soul's Openner

A Bundle of Tales

The tale about the soul is a tale about the invisible; revealing that which cannot be touched and thus, told through numerous tales, all of which are attestation to the glimpses of it, not always seen with our naked eyes. A tale may lead to another, or stand on its own. It is like meeting your beloved briefly, only to let go and want to be together once more.

I was walking on the shoreline, just by the water, hearing the music of the waves that were almost touching my feet, being one with it, forgetting all else and moving to its rhythm – like in a walking meditation; I was contemplating the question about our soul, and thought to call it – 'that, which will never die', only others referred to it too, as the non-loss that exists in creation where, all is transformed, but never lost, energy to form to energy – and back again, and again.

That, which will never die that I refer to here, is the Eternal, the Constant, the Absolute - it is the same force instilled in us during our creation, the Living Divine Soul, which is ancient and eternal forever.

Even at moments when one thinks one is about to die, or that cannot go on, the rhythm of this Divine Spark is still sounding in us. Even when eventually we are passing on from life in this world, we do not die, because the 'we' in us is this Divine Spark, it returns to the Light of the Creator, and our body to the Earth. The physical transforms and renewed for further physical manifestations, but the Divine Spark is Light forever more, never changing, just inviting new experiences in different forms.

We are never lost, and we are forever useful and important. Through our active and inactive times, through our joys and grieves, through every breathe and every thought, feeling, knowing and silent moment, we are living thus, we exist thus, we are required to breath-on this Divine Spark and feel its glory – and honour it throughout.

Relate to each moment, as a new beginning, and it will become for you another tale of your journey. Collect these tales and thread them together, like a string of pearls, each beautiful and valued for its own sake, and all are beautiful together, as a necklace – as the treasured story of your life.

If you ask me to tell you my tales, they are far too many. It is not as important to tell them, as to understand their existence and importance, and this is what I am here to share with you.

What are we – if but a dream
What are we – if not to carry the flame
The flame of Light and Love
We are it – the Oneness of it all.

4

Spiritual Place of Seclusion

Now, in order to allow the glimpses to show themselves, and for us to be in a more of a perceptive state, let us find the *Spiritual Place of Seclusion*. Your spiritual place of seclusion could be a spot to sit on a vast shore, or a moment of silence within your heart on a busy day.

This place could be anywhere and any time that you can indulge yourself in the privacy of your being, without the commotion or penetration of your environment – like drawing into the eye of the storm.

It is a strange thing, as we draw quiet and still, we may discover that which we really are. It is like we have a small flame in our hearts – barely seen and barely felt, but quietness and stillness suddenly flare it larger.

You ask yourself, was the flame there before, but you know the answer, because you felt it so.

The Divine Spark in us is a spark of flame, you may envisage it as a candle flame, and when you draw silent and still, you may envisage it growing and enlarging to be like The Burning Bush that is never consumed. Let this burning bush engulf your whole being, enlighten you, as well as protect you.

Within it, you are now secluded, so let it be your spiritual place of seclusion.

There is a special thing to remember and understand, while trying to understand the need for a spiritual place of seclusion, you see, that which is obvious may be loud and gross, but that which is sublime and private will always be delicate and soft – just like a whisper.

Our minds, feelings and emotions, usually are very active, and leave no space for privacy, nor for anything that will denote only us – in a singular term. Our minds are always measuring things by reference points, so you are always seen in reference to others.

The fascinating point of interest is that when you are contemplating in silence, you immediately feel that although, you are there by yourself, you are not alone, and that which is with you is unidentifiable!

The whole of creation is within you, held in trust due to that that you are a very important part of it. You have designated vocation and purpose, and you are one very significant component of creation.

Therefore, it is necessary that while acknowledging it, you will take the time to enter your spiritual place of seclusion, so you may connect to it, and be your own authentic self.

Clue number one will be that you must drop and let go of all judgement, towards others and towards yourself.

Just Be.

Sit quietly amidst the noise
Breathe deeply within your heart
Can you feel it?
Your inner self is calling to you now.

The Ultimate Sublime
&
The Truth-Resonance-Gong

The 'Ultimate Sublime', the one which is sublime to my mind, but known to my heart, The One, The Creator of The Truth, who I carry in my heart of hearts, to be the 'Truth Indeed'.

This is what our soul knows; it knows no lies, no exaggerations, and no inaccuracies. Our soul is beyond stories, because it knows the Truth. This is why it is so hard for people to meet their true selves. The discrepancy between what they think they are, and what they really are, is so immense that it frightens them to look within. They forgot that there is no judgment when the creature returns to the creator – its source, there is only unconditional love.

I have mentioned in my book of The Essential Key to Wisdom, how I related to it. I imagined a gong in my heart. I called it the *Truth-Resonance-Gong*. Each step I took, each person I met, each book I picked up even before reading it, each experience looming on my personal horizon, practically – each and every moment and all it contained – I let it create its own unique sound on my gong thus, revealing the truth of it and in it – if it existed at all.

I let my *Truth-Resonance-Gong* help me determine the Rightness of things, so I may carry on my way to my destination – to fulfill my own Vocation.

You see, in the light of Truth, the Ultimate Sublime basks freely, and as you are the Divine Spark, you may bask in it too.

I might like to elaborate some more about this, but truth be told, it is something that experience makes it known, rather than understanding it with you mind. The level of Truth that is in our being is held on a cellular level, and one must be attuned, pause a bit, and only then decide if to respond to any stimuli.

What if the whole of your being has a silent scream of 'beware', do you stop, do you listen, and do you change your direction?

Surely, you have felt exhilaration before, may it be because of a person, or an occasion. What did you inner self try to tell you?

Have you ever woke up from a dream and knew what that day will bring?

Will you admit that many a times you knew in advance what the outcome will be, but continued nevertheless?

The *Truth-Resonance-Gong* is an ally, a friend and a tool, given to us – with great love – to use.

The promise is that the Ultimate Sublime will always be truthful to you. If you meet with untruth – you have listened to lesser things.

Inner-self-trust may be developed by taking the time and making the effort to listen to your inner truth. You, too, are equipped with the *Truth-Resonance-Gong*.

The reason its service is not always promoted is so others will have control over you, but do you want that?

In my booklet The 7 Pillars Your Authentic Self Stands On I specifically defined your birth rights and gifts, it is important that you will feel that you are as rich, and use them.

The Light shown softly in my heart of hearts
The flame floated on the lake within
The waters are so calm, deep and blue
And I have known peace within it all.

Assimilation of Realization

We are coming now to a very important concept, understanding it, will lead us all to knowing.

Knowing our soul and its true nature and substance requires us to look properly. I once wrote and defined it thus:

"Assimilation of realization can only occur if your perception gave birth to understanding."

What does it mean?

In the first six months of a baby's life, the baby only observes, his perception is acute, but he has not yet assimilated it. Like a baby, even an adult faced with any new subject and information about it, cannot draw on it before he will assimilate it – absorb it, to a level whereby, he will suddenly realize and grasp its meaning and thus, will understand it. Therefore, we may say, that until a person understands something, which is entirely new to him, he has not yet realized its meaning and therefore, did not yet assimilate his perception.

There are times that our general understanding of life deepens, what happens then is that certain things that were understood before, are now re-assimilated and a new understanding is gained. This is a very important point, because it illustrates that nothing, but for The Truth, is cast in stone and unchangeable. It is far safer to state that 'at this time, with the current level of understanding, I understand that…' versus, 'this is it – no arguments please.'

Although, this seems somewhat complex, it is of a vital importance, because it is the root of all of our self-imposed sufferings. By that I mean if we do not realize properly that which we perceived, we are bound to understand it wrongly and thus, be hurt, or angry, or any other feeling on a long list of negative feelings.

Let us say that we were in an experience that left us bitter. Undoubtedly, there are numerous psychological explanations or personality studies that will provide us with some reasoning, but firstly, it all dependents on the fact that we forgot who we really are, what we are here for in life, and what our power is.

You see, the Divine Spark also denotes that which you are. You are part of The Light of The Creator therefore, although different in degree, you are still the same as the source – you carry the same Truth, as your substance and sustenance.

If I will put two mirrors in front of you, each of a different type of clarity, the first mirror will show the reflection that caused you bitterness, the second mirror will show the reflection of the Truth – can you see how your image in them will differ?

Have you ever been to those carnivals and fairs that had a mirror room, which contained different mirrors, each reflecting differently, distorting the actual, like one that makes you appear taller, or fatter, or concave, or convex, and so on? This is what I mean by having different reflections, but only one can be the True Reflection – The Reflection of The Truth.

Well, when dealing with reflection rather than reality, one is bound to make errors. That is not to say that it is an easy thing to decipher the real reality, but should that be an excuse not to be looking for it?

I propose to you this, if you intend to live a truthful life, which will have true joy in it, you should make a commitment to yourself that you will do your utmost to discern the true reality namely, let go of false pretences, let go of fears and doubts, fill your heart and mind with the knowing that you are not alone and that you are immensely important, have courage to live life to the full, despite any and all limitations. Then you will find that the Real Reality will seek you, you will see it almost in every corner, on every face, and in every flower.

Reality is not elusive; it is our sight which is. If the tool is inaccurate, then the tool is to be re-calibrated. Re-calibrating our sight depends on our perception and the assimilation of it.

Another very important tool-accuracy-bending-conditioner is our belief systems, may they be community based, or personal. Our belief systems are add-ons in life, they are not really necessary in order to live life to the full. True living actually may be achieved by relating to each moment, person, occurrence and such, as a newly created thing. As a matter of fact, everything is new, there are no equal moments in life, nor any person is the same as he was a moment ago.

Our bodies regenerate themselves every second; it could be that in less than a year, your whole body replaced itself with new cells. You might look the same, but you consist of different particles.

Our minds change easily with every experience we are going through, so what we were a moment before it, is no longer.

Let us say that yesterday all was fine and today, suddenly, you won the Lottery. Surely, you will feel differently? Although, it is born of a relative reference, you are indeed different to the person of yesterday. It is the set of belief systems that leads many of those who won the Lottery, to lose it all, it is not their capability of being rich.

What for our consciousness
What for realization
We are, and must be
And our key is understanding

Belief Systems & Our Soul

Imagine this; you are a crystal glass, only your soul, not wine, fills this glass. Your soul is radiant and made of pure light thus, it suppose to shine through this beautiful crystal glass. Alas, the glass has smudges on it from unclean hands who handled it, so you cannot see the light, you cannot see the soul.

Once I have heard a story of the dance of the seven veils well, the story might have had different theme entwined in it, but I would like to use this dance as an allegory.

Imagine that you dance a soul-searching dance where you invite your soul to reveal itself to you. Imagine that you remove one veil after another, in meditative slow movements full of gentility and grace until, there, your soul's glory is all there before you.

A dance like this is to be performed daily, it takes dedication, love and trust, as well as repetition to achieve the revealing of the soul once, and then many times more, but when you do, you will not have any doubt whatsoever to whom you are, and how important you are.

Let us ask then, what are those veils, what are you removing to reveal (not expose) your soul. An important point of understanding is required here, between revealing and exposing. Exposing denotes becoming unsecured and unprotected whereby, revealing denotes removal of that which makes you insecure and unprotected, so you may touch upon the essence of your truth and draw courage from it, like revealing a treasure. You may want to look upon it, as the pleasantness when a cloud cover is cleared from the sky, the sky is now blue, the sun is shining and there is nothing that stands between you.

It is not to be taken lightly, the influence of a lack or abundance of sun light to the health of people on Earth, so one should learn from it and understand that the light of our soul is as required for our good overall health, as the sun light, if not more.

Back to the veils, I call veils all which are unnecessary add-ons. Our belief systems are a mechanism that was instilled in us to understand how to survive in nature. The mechanism is defining reference points and your position in relation to them. For example, you would expect to perform duties that required light and the use of your eye sight mostly during the day. The heart of the fire is beautiful, but very hot, so you don't voluntarily put your hand in it. On a cold winter day, you will dress up warmly before going out, so you may come back, and will not turn to a statue of ice on the way.

You may ask, so what went wrong? Well, fear came in and distorted the reflections and therefore, many more reference points were added on, which were exaggerated needlessly.

We have landed up having many more belief systems than are needed. That created separation among people and unfortunately, it has also created an inner separation, between us and our souls.

You remember I have said that each and every one of us has the Divine Spark within them, and that this Divine Spark is of the Divine thus, each and every one of us is connected to the Divine, like molecules in a large body that are forming the body.

For this reason, if by having a specific belief system we create a separation, and go ahead and attack other people, in actuality we harm ourselves.

This is why the concept of harmony exists. Wherever you witness harmony, you witness peace and goodwill. Wherever harmony is absent, you witness strife, so one should understand that separation will breed strife while, collaboration will breed harmony.

Our belief systems are really entrenched in us, as they were created on all levels, the personal, family, immediate community, the nation, and the whole of Humanity. A family would tell you not to reveal something to your neighbours, for fear of ridicule, as much as Humanity will envisage beings from outer space, as harmful and dangerous.

Studies that were made to research adopted children, comparing the influence of their environment on their development, also revealed that sometimes, some of the children will respond in manners, which they could only attribute to a genetic influence.

If you look at yourself now, and understand that the whole of your being, which includes your physical body, comprises also your belief systems, and if like excess weight, you would understand that it is much better to rid yourself of the excess belief systems, would you do it?

I hope that you answered with a big resonating yes, because the next stage is really trying to identify them, and living a life which is more realistic and authentic.

Standing on a vast shore
My soul felt one with the sea
Alas, my person was looking to and fro
Trying to shake it all - to see

Finding & Redefining

The Divine Truth is an absolute and a constant hence, our truth is relative. If you understand that, you will also understand that the relative may be questioned.

Something happened in your day, or life and you responded in a certain way. Late that night, in the privacy of your heart and thought, you may ask yourself what were the thoughts and feelings that made you respond, or react, in the manner that you did. Good or bad, that is not the point, what matters is understanding if what you thought and felt was true, or was it bred of fear, or any other negative manifestation.

A child, unfortunately, has not yet developed common sense, knowledge and knowing in order to distinguish exactly between what he is told, which most of the times will be a relative truth, to what he might feel intuitively to be the truth. Adults, most of the times, try to limit a child, due to their own apprehensions.

You, like all of us, were conditioned in that way from the moment of your conception, birth and until now. Actually, seven veils might be too few; some of us may have to take off heavy coats.

Do not despair. Our soul shines the truth at all times. Our soul and the Divine Spark within us are here to help us every moment of every day throughout our lives, they do not waiver.

It is your resolution they need. If you are resolute to live by the Truth, to honour your Divine Self and your soul, your spirit will rise and you will gain steadfastness in your life.

Please do not resort to 'How to' solutions, as the only means to discover The Truth. Please listen within, as your connection to it is constant, you just have to realize it.

Let us say that a person, in this day and age, who is used to be 'instructed' rather than be 'inventive', would like to find out more about their specific belief-system's makeup. Well, if you ever read some biographies you would know that they are good examples, as they practically list the conditions and responses of that person's life.

Therefore, you could start writing your own, not by creating a novel unless you wish to, but by listing, even in a bullet form, what seem to be the facts and events of your life.

Slowly but surely, you will see several patterns forming up. It will also show you what your personality, in any specific age relating to a specific event, might have been, which will also teach you a lot about the belief systems you held at the time.

That is right, your belief systems do not have to exist throughout your life sometimes though, a few of them will. We change belief systems as we grow in age, knowledge, wisdom, self-confidence and self-esteem. You might even see, or hear about, a marvellous creation that will inspire you so, that your belief system might shift, and you will not be the same anymore.

The important point is to make it simpler. What do I mean by it?

Well, think about your belief systems as a luggage you have to carry, day in and day out. The more you have, the more you have to carry and consider. Your system will automatically delegate most of it to your sub-conscious, to make things more fluid, fast and second-nature.

Can you imagine how much your sub-conscious may be burdened with?

Your sub-conscious also happens to take care of the majority of your body's processors, as well as that it never rests, so the burden would indeed be too heavy, and something might therefore, be compromised.

Any time that any part of you is compromised, you will not be able to live to the full, your health might be challenged as well, and indeed you will suffer. Yet, it is unnecessary to suffer in such a way, so let us make it simpler.

A small and much known example would be from our physical realm, when we have a cold or flu, or any such regularly occurring inconvenience, we immediately prompted by our bodies to minimize our food intake – making it simpler for the body to concentrate its efforts toward healing itself.

Consequently, is it not easy to believe that having a simpler 'diet of the mind' will help us better than being with a more complex one?

When looking and finding your own belief systems, sometimes you will be faced with an issue of loyalty and faithfulness. What do I mean by that?

If your parent, country, religion, or any such important figure in your life, is the one that induced in you a specific belief system that actually damages your life rather than improves it, letting it go might make you feel rebellious and disloyal.

Even more than that, when they discover that you have changed your belief, they might actually blame you as such. It is of a vital importance to have then the courage to assert what is right for you, and very gently and respectfully state that you are entitled to your own set of beliefs.

You see, the Truth is only one thus, all relative truths are just that – relative, and if you explain it, it will be better received.

I once had such a case, and decided to use a metaphor from another subject to illustrate it better. I said to my friend that if we will both take ten different artists and bring them to the same spot in nature, and ask them to paint the sunset, as it was happening right there and then, we will get ten different paintings, each conceived by the seeing eyes of a specific artist.

Would we be able to blame them and say, can you not see the same sunset? No, we could not, because of the very simple fact, that each and every one of them comes from a different background, personality, eye-sight, and yes, belief systems.

If we would then take those ten paintings and exhibit them in an art gallery, they would all be valued and admired, by different people, to different degrees.

Now, can you tell me that any one of those artist was unfaithful to nature and the sunset?

Of course not.

The only faithfulness that you must put first on your priority list is the one to The Creator and The Divine Spark within you, all other, take second place.

When you live life like that, you will discover a marvellous thing. When you ask others to respect your right to exist and be truthful to yourself, it will also be very easy for you to grant them the same. It will bring freedom to your relationships, because you would not be placing yourself in control-issue conflicts.

This will denote to you, and to the world, that which you perceive to be your value.

In a room full of mirrors
My image was covered from head to toe
I noticed then the light and warmth
And gingerly took off my heavy coat

Understanding Your Value

There were many philosophers and poets through the ages, who delighted us with the fruits of their muse. Some of them were so brilliant that they outshine all the rest of us, but does it mean that 'your song' is not good enough because of it?

Another example is that at one point in my life, I distinguished between the prayers used for generations and the prayers I uttered. There is nothing that can compete with the psalms written by King David, but with a humble heart I wrote a couple myself, not to replace, but to add on.

Like this today, I feel about the words of a song written by another. I love singing, which means that, many times, I would sing songs that someone else composed and wrote, but are their words mine, do they really express what I feel, or am I transposing myself to their experience, and not living my own?

Your soul can be torn between someone else's relative truth, and your own. If your soul does not utter its own words, may it be in opinion, song, or prayer, it will always be torn, and your truth will never be expressed.

Understanding your value means that you understand that you were not created by chance, or by a whim, you were created with purpose and value. Therefore, it is of an utmost importance for you to understand your value.

It is quite fine to read books, poems, and sing songs, even pray with other people's words, as long as you do it with awareness and observation. The awareness will allow you to remind yourself that you are using the other person's words, at this time, and that you are aware they are not yours. For example, when I recite psalm 23 from the Bible, I am aware that its meaning is symbolic to me, and I am drawing on King David's true love to God to inspire me too. I remind myself that even a king acknowledged The Higher King and asked for goodness to be bestowed on him.

Observation is necessary in order that you will be able to see where the differences lie. Where you are borrowing, and ask yourself if you could have been more authentic, at that time. You may observe a certain difference that will lead you to understand your situation better and thus, might even inspire you and highlight to you your next action step.

Most of the times, all that our soul asks of us is to be aware of its existence, power and importance. It is like your parents allowed you to go out when young, but wanted you to remember which home is yours, and come back to it. Knowing what and where your home is and then taking action to come back to it, instils in you stability, security, and a higher self-esteem. This also creates a better sense of direction therefore, your heart will be more courageous and ready for action.

I know that, at times, people did not get the right messages at home, with regard to their value, if any. I know that for many, home will be considered a painful subject while others, will not want to leave it at all. One must take all in stride; we are talking here of an optimal home environment.

Our value is not determined by our families, society, riches, or anything of this Earth. Our value is evident because we exist. I love the saying that St. Francis de Sales, who lived in the 16th century, said, and I quote: "Have patience with all things but first with yourself. Never confuse your mistakes with your value as a Human Being. You're a perfectly valuable, creative, worthwhile person simply because you exist. And no amount of triumphs or tribulations can ever change that. Unconditional self acceptance is the core of a peaceful mind."

I would add to it that no matter what others say about your value, they did not grant it, nor can they revoke it. It is of a vital importance to understand that, because that releases you from other people's mercy, and allows you to be a person of your own.

One of the more painful veils to remove is the veils created by the lessons and challenges we took upon ourselves.

I have to set a premise here; our soul has chosen to be born and to evolve in a certain way. That way required our soul to challenge itself, so it may go through a learning curve, at the end of which it would have gained a very comprehensive knowledge and experience about that specific issue, healed from it, and is able to help others with similar issues.

You may ask, so what happens in between? Well, we have an added complication, because these lessons and challenges, most of the times, obscure the Truth, so we may walk blindly and stumble often.

If you think of yourself as a sea faring vessel, you will have to use sails, or engine to power yourself, but you will also have to use some kind of a rudder, or controls, to set out your azimuth – your direction, so when you apply power to it, you will move in the direction you want to move toward.

What our lessons and challenges bring are storms, power cuts, broken parts and so on, which all are doing the same thing – they distract you from proceeding in the right direction.

It is only your keen heart, which will yearn to go in the right direction, which will yearn to get there already, that will induce in you the doubt, that you may have been distracted.

This is why it is so important to acknowledge your own worth, importance and identification – to get back on the right path, and have the courage to carry on walking on it despite the distractions.

You remember that I said that the lessons are necessary for our soul's growth ability, so you may see now that it is not important to lay blame for them, it is important to acknowledge that you were distracted, take a deep breathe, and go back to the designated direction.

At the beginning of this book, I put one of the sayings I composed:

"If you believe your destination,

             you become your goal."

This is what I mean by it, if you know your heart, you will know your purpose and vocation, which they could be multiple and not necessarily singulars. If you will put your purpose and vocation at the forefront of your mind, you will then set the goal to adjust, grow and develop yourself to the level where you can reach them – fulfill them.

You, who comprise the whole of your being, including your belief systems, will have to participate, so it is you that you will work on.

The eagle was listening attentively
And I looked up and saw it
A love bird was singing a song
That brought forth the dawn

What Is Our Work?

This is the question, and a very simple one at that.

The work that our soul took upon itself is actually the sum of all that our soul meant to learn in this lifetime while, achieving and fulfilling the purpose and vocation it took upon itself.

In addition, the work of the person, who is the house and temple of the soul on this Earth, is to clear the way to connect with the soul and thus, become the True Vessel that shines the light of the soul through, without any obstructions.

Life experiences, challenges and lessons, become then 'life's expressions', which are beautiful in themselves, even if some of them are of suffering. You see, an expression is just that, it is not the substance or the actual – it is just an expression.

When using the same terminology to different degrees, because our vocabulary and lexicons allow us just so many words, one should understand how a word becomes applicable, or not to a situation.

For example, in order to live on this Earth, in this day and age, one must work in some kind of way that brings financial remuneration. Going to work therefore, cannot be equal to the work that the soul and the person are to do in this life time, they differ in kind and in degree.

If though, you decide to work in a job that is one and the same as your vocation, for example, a teacher, composer, writer, and builder and so on, then 'your work' brings double-gain.

People, who allow their work environment to use all of their resources, in any case will not have much of a 'life' and thus, will not have much of a chance to work at their purpose and vocation, as well as their personal growth.

This is the main reason in understanding that it is of a vital importance to differentiate between the shades and degrees of meanings of words.

A word's meaning creates expectations, definitions and conceptual understanding. If one is not accurate about it there will be a major opening for disasters. Some disasters ended up being the material for comedy shows, but that is only because many a times we try to laugh at our mistakes, in order not to lose faith in life.

We should have been taught in school, right from kindergarten to matriculation, how to look at life, and how to define shades of word's meanings.

Did you ever notice how many shades of green are there in nature? Our world is based on versatility, abundance and differentiation, and not on narrow mindedness. Our speech, in itself, asks us to be colourful and imaginative, so why not allow it?

If therefore, you define life as an opportunity to achieve fulfillment of your purpose and vocation, Then you must clear all obstructions from having a good continuous connection with your soul, and become the True Vessel of the Light, you can then call this opportunity 'the innocency of life', as the intent of life has no design to harm you.

This is so indeed. All that your soul took upon itself, and that you live through, is free of any malicious thought and design. All is within a sublime idea of the greatness your soul may achieve; if it can, with you, be strengthened to be its own best.

Hence, your work, in the greater

scheme of things, should become your focus and destination. Thereafter, you, the person that may help it all to be and manifest, will become your goal.

You may understand from this how much smaller in degree your day to day work, or job, is, and that it is of a vital importance to acknowledge it as so. For all the people that are stressed out, because of what is going on in their place of work, I would say: please remember that this place, these people and these problems will not exist in the not too far future, but your soul and their souls will last for eternity.

Let the business of life be like storms at sea; let your vessel traverse the waters, gliding assuredly to your destination. Remember that you are greater than anyone, including yourself, suspects.

Be resolute, and work to be your best.

What am I to do, I asked
And I heard a whisper: dance
What dance is that to be
And my soul answered: mine

Faith

Faith is not to be mistaken with religious thoughts, feelings and concepts.

Yes, in religion you also need faith, but I am referring here to a far more vital type of faith.

Going back to visit our baby, have you ever asked yourself what is that thing that motivates the baby to always bounce back, to always arrive back at a level of contentment?

Please remember that I am talking here too about a baby that lives in 'acceptable' conditions. Even though, babies who are born to hardship, show resilience and ability to bounce back, far more easily than their adult counterparts.

The baby is born with the innate knowing of

what life is namely, life is work. The baby will not shy away from extending its efforts, or maintaining openness of heart. The baby, in a way, is like a flower that will grow and bloom regardless of the weather's surprises, may it be a late snow or thunder shower. The flower may show its bloom for a minute or a day yet, it fulfilled its vocation, even then.

Faith, in this context, is the resilient knowing that life is a flow and work. Life is to be taken anew, each and every moment of it, there should be no taking for granted, or living on an auto-pilot.

I was trying to think of how to help people distinguish this type of faith, from their religious one, and thought to try using it as an acronym to some meaningful words, for example:

*F*ully

*A*ttributed

*I*ntelligent

*T*ruth's

*H*ome.

In life, you may find beauty, if you are looking for vitality, liveliness, and newness, but even the dormant may be beautiful.

The dormant may also be mistaken for the unseen. The unseen may be unseen due to our limited eye-sight ability, or that it depends on our ability to conceive it. The unseen may also be fleeting, or it may be beyond the realm of life on Earth.

All that we do not see, or do not know, does not stop our inner authentic self from yearning for it.

What holds us on in life is our innate faith.

The sun was shining on a new day
And I was awakened full of vitality
The next day, the rain had come
And I was awakened to the promise

The Beauty

I once set on a beach, basking in the spring's sun, when I was transposed to another level of seeing, and feeling. I tried to capture it in words, as much as I could in that state of mind, and I would like to share it with you.

The Beauty

Streaming as rivers from mountain tops thus, is the beauty streaming down to Earth. Free from form, free from duty, direct impression of God's almighty love to her creatures. God is thy giver and love is her tool. Only purity and simplicity free of form.

Why free of form?

So it can be received by any vessel of any

shape and any size.

So it can penetrate any surface, any shell.

So it will not be free to be defined or formed.

So it can carry on flowing from the receiving vessel to yet another one.

Also, it will not harden in a form and only some evidence of its fleeting presence will find its way in expression of elation described in any form of art or expression derived from that touch of beauty awakening the human heart.

The beauty is the expression of love and the proof of giving, and blessed they be that can recognize it.

Have you witnessed a face glowing with elation, high in the discovery? You have seen the beauty then, of the soul that has just seen the light and touch of God — strong in the conviction of its rightness.

Have you seen two moments equal in the beauty? Of course not, because no vessel is equal to another thus, no expression is identical.

Please live life moment to moment. Feel the beauty of every moment and fill yourself with its uniqueness.

*On those days when your heart is in pain,
know that it lacks this beauty, so visualize
the rich waters of beauty streaming down
to Earth from God's heart, know yourself
to be a capable vessel and receive freely,
then give freely.*   (©2000 ISBN 0-9781498-8-2)

Have faith. Have patience with yourself and with others. Live life – it is your work.

And let us continue discovering the way to the Soul's Openner.

What a wonderful game life has for us

Look here, look there, look everywhere

The Divine Beauty was revealed

As we looked into the deep

Hope

Please read this poem first, I wrote it on a day that one of my challenges presented itself to me, and I let my heart speak thus first:

Hope

The ancient blessed Hope

Was born on a day that uncertainty

Gave birth to despair and pain,

Pain that touched our Father's heart

The heart, which felt compassion for our hearts

That felt compassion for his own heart in observing

The troubled road that our life

Let us walk on

That we, without knowing, walked on

As if there was no other

Is there no other?

The path that brought difficulties

The path that was full of obstacles

Obstacles that were created on the same day

Our Father granted us Free Will

Without us being blessed with wisdom

Even if we strive to find it

Why isn't life blessed with simplicity

Simplicity that brings grace

That gives birth to beauty and blessings

And love reigns then on all.

Those are hard question unless, you take them in context with what I have written up until now, as well as the name of this piece – Hope.

It was said that all the troubles came to the world when Pandora opened her box, but there was one last small thing that was there in the box as well – the hope. It was hope that made it possible to live, and carry on living.

I relate this hope to the Faith I spoke of in a previous chapter. One is derivative of the other, and both are mutually connected.

It is because the prime intent for us in life is to fulfill our purpose and vocation while, advancing on the path of our personal growth, that we must have faith and hope.

We are meant to live while alive, and not only survive. We are meant to be active, positive, and industrious. We are meant to bear fruit; our heart will not let us rest and will plea with us to listen and quench its thirst.

If we were doomed from the start, not even one ray of sunshine will bring a smile to our faces and warm our hearts. No baby will be born, and the species will cease to exist, or would have already a long time ago.

It does not matter how many wars, nuclear disasters or bombs, accidents and what not, Humanity still goes on – still exists and is so many billions strong.

There are people who live at the footsteps of volcanoes that live through their eruptions, and still come back, build again and live to see another day. What drives them on if not Faith, Hope, and a wishful heart yearning for this home.

Will you rise above the mundane to see that life has got a far greater meaning? I want you to, because I would like to see you opening up to your soul, and all its gifts.

The innocency of life and its consistency
The eyes of a babe who was just fed
Laughter and joy as his embrace
Warming our heart, when in despair

The Path
Joy versus Hardship

There are some who think that all is predestined, and there are those that think that it all depends on what you make out of your own life. I would like you to ask your inner-self the following questions:

Why is it that I was created: what for, how, and do I matter?

It is because I believe indeed that each and every one of us is created for their own unique reason, that I acknowledge the importance of all beings, and all parts of Creation.

Think of yourself as a drop of water in the river of Creation. The river may flow, advance and be, due to the sum of all of its drops. The water is the amalgamation of the drops, but the movement is the amalgamation of their intent. The flow will be determined by how united their intents are – stagnation can only occur when there is not enough force to create the flow.

The direction of the flow is always one, as much as rivers flow to the sea, and only at the sea level do they take on a different type flow, so is Creation.

A drop of the river's water may not 'wish' to join the flow of that river, or may choose to be of a different use, but either way the drop exercises a choice, and eventually it will arrive at the sea.

A Human-Being may choose to be of service to Humanity, or take part in the growth of Humanity, or alas, can choose not to be part of it. Regardless, Humanity will still advance, grow, and develop.

Therefore, understanding that which is uniquely us, our vocations, purposes and skills, is a key for us to know what are we coming to the 'flow' with, and how we may join our intent to the whole.

This is the way to actually discover what your path is, as your path is the only ground that will support you in achieving it all.

Your path though, will have a theme to it, to

be precise; it will have one of two available themes.

You may walk, learn and advance on the path of hardship, or you may choose to do it on the path of joy. You may also re-choose along the way, as you are not bound to the theme, but by your own choice making.

You see, we do have to go through the lessons and challenges in order to help our soul achieve that which it set out to achieve, but we may separately choose as to how we do it.

Unfortunately, Humanity, somewhere in the timeline when people decided to settle down in larger communities, converted their thinking of what life is, and opened up the stage for a new term − suffering.

I am quite sure that in bygone ages, people knew life is work, and did not shy from it. I am also quite sure that when people started living a life where their supplies became more abundant, due to storage facilities and planning, they started looking at the 'work' of life with different eyes, they judged it do be a 'burden'.

With the introduction of a new look at life, burden gave birth to suffering and then to hardship.

These days, people measure what they do not have, as they go hurriedly in comparing themselves to others. They also set up goals and aspirations in that way, the way to 'have more'.

People forgot that the walk on their path to fulfilling their vocation is to be their most important priority.

You can easily understand that if one becomes distracted by additional, unnecessary arguments, one may collapse under it, rather then arrive at the finish line.

We can see, that even here, simplicity is the key for peace of mind and heart, so how does the path of joy differ from the path of hardship?

The term 'to be content' is born of lake of hardship, or what we believe hardship to be. The term 'a wise person' is born from one who took upon themselves to understand the difference between things, including the difference between true necessities, and seemingly ones.

If you ask yourself, prior to making assumptions, is a specific thing actually needed in your life, or does it just belong to the 'nice to have' category, and arrive at an answer, which is authentic to your being – and not to your belief systems, conditioning and society pressures, you may proceed by allowing yourself to make a true choice in having it or not, working for it or not, actually, enslaving yourself to it or not.

The path of hardship will include in it all these add-ons that force you to work far harder and many times, in different directions than the one leading you to your destination. In this path, you may become bitter and dismayed at not feeling fulfilled and successful.

The hardship path is a path that you do not have the last say in. On this path, loneliness will be your constant companion. This path may also lead you to aloneness.

On the other hand, the path of joy allows you to feel joy in all that you do (to the best of your current and fluid ability), and to proceed with a content heart.

On the path of joy, you will know that your destination is clear, you are a free person to choose the interruptions on your way and how you respond to them. You will not hold grudges, nor feel jealousy. You will feel that your fellow man is entitled to the same consideration, and you will not try to force yourself on anyone, nor be their slave. If anyone else will try to enforce themselves on you, you will gracefully bid them goodbye, and turn to carry on your way to your destination.

The path of joy will bring you more friendships

and alliances, as others will not be repelled by your oversized competitive nature, nor will you threaten them in any way.

The difference between these two path-themes, will also determines how much energy, clarity, and ability you will have to proceed in your life, personal growth and purpose.

You see, as fewer interruptions you will have, as easier it will be for you to focus, and the intensity of your focusing, will allow you to advance faster.

It is very clear that the manner in which you relate to our life, will direct you to choose the theme of your path. Hardship or joy will lead you with more or less meandering, to your destination.

Which way would you like to take?

The wind died down and silence instilled
The waves subsided, and all was calm
I then saw it right before me
The path to my destination

Aids to the Unveiling

In the theatre, you have a role to play and the costume to go with it. Usually, as greater an actor you are, as more people you will have to attend to you, and help you in both putting on your costume, and taking it off.

In the theatre, you are aware of the role you are about to play, and at the end of the play, you know that you will have to shed it off. If you have just played Hamlet's wife, you cannot imagine that you can come out and carry on killing people in the streets.

Alas, in the theatre of life, it is not entirely the same.

Our environment, nation, religion, gender, and family endow us with multiple costumes. Fears, formed throughout life, will endow us with some more, but it is up to us to understand it all, and to act upon it.

It is us, whom are required to call off the role duration, differentiating between them, and their importance. It is up to us to know, which costume is really a costume, and is it damaging or helping us, and so on.

Up until now, I mentioned a number of things that are essential aids, but they are given aids. For example, we are born with Faith and Hope, and unless someone suffers from depression, they will be visible and usable provided you have the willingness to acknowledge them. Otherwise, a person with depression will have to take some steps to elevate the depression somewhat in order for these given aids to become visible. They are there, trust that, but they must also be visible in order to be used. The Human mind tends to forget that, which it does not regularly see.

Hence, the given aids are our soul, the *Truth-Resonance-Gong*, our value, faith, the beauty, hope, joy, and our ability to observe and discern, and, of course, we need to add to this – all that life, nature and the Divine bestow on us daily.

In addition to these aids, we may use others to help us unveil – reveal our soul.

The most important one of all is our willingness.

We cannot move forward in life without our willingness to do so.

Our willingness may come in many shapes, but the key is that whatever we give sanction to, becomes a form of our willingness. Please understand this, every relationship requires two or more sides. Even in an unspeakable circumstances, somewhere along the line, a sanction was given, may it be knowingly or not. This is why we need to be using all of our faculties to discern the truth, and act upon it.

You can see why it is so important for you to define your destination and believe in it with all your heart. How else would you be able to focus upon yourself and your betterment?

We even know of people that have been in dire circumstances that vowed to get out of it – and did. The difference between them and those who have not gotten away was their power of belief in themselves and their truth.

Thus, first have willingness.

Secondly, you need to perform self-searching, so you may get in touch with your truth, faith and hope. For this, you may utilize the *Spiritual Place of Seclusion* – wherever you are. Your inner self is your sanctuary, and awaits you continuously.

Thirdly, you need to define your destination and work on your belief in it. A vital important test may be incorporated here to validate the truth of the destination, ask yourself each day if your destination is what it is truly, be courageous and acknowledge the truth. Usually, for all the days of your life, your true destination will resound in you strongly, and this test will just make it stronger.

Next, you need to engage your inner observer to its full capacity, in order to allow you to define the roles you took upon yourself to play, and specifically, while you play them.

Let me illustrate it to you by using the analogy of the Marionettes. The marionettes are puppets used to convey a story to a young audience, by having them move physically while, a voice narrates the story.

The essential point here is that the puppets are just performing the physical portion, and not by their own will, as they are attached to strings that are controlled by others.

The marionettes are not portrayed as having consciousness, or free will. They do not exercise their power of choice. The listeners know that they are moved by the strings attached.

Unlike them, we are Human-Beings with a fully fledged free will. We are able, even if only inwardly, to exercise our consciousness and free will – we are able to determine our own destiny, by choosing our destination.

The difference between our true destination and our currently understood one is that our true destination will call us to it while, it is with our whim that we will choose the latter.

When you activate your inner observer, you can see your life as a puppet show. It will be very clear to you then, when you are true to yourself, and when you are not. When you achieve understanding, you reach knowing. You will know when it is a role you play versus allowing your soul to shine. Many of the roles create an impression that we must be non-stop involved, but here too there are boundaries, which will keep us in a healthy zone, or outside of it. We will talk some more about boundaries later on.

Next, you must give up judgement and fear, and induce love instead.

When you are based in love, you are able to act correctly. There is a difference between Right Action and just an action. It is the same difference that there is between responding and reacting, it is all evident in the consequences.

Imagine that you are engaged in an argument, try and step out into the observer's stand and ask yourself, why are you in this argument? What is it that you are trying to achieve, and do you have the mandate to affect it.

Previously, when I discussed the differentiation between the paths of joy to the one of hardship, I mentioned that a major clue will be to let go of judgement.

When you are observing yourself in an argument, or even a quarrel, you are able then to also observe where you are based. Are you based in judgement, fear or love? The mirrors of judgement and fear will always distort the true reality while, the mirror of love will allow you to release and let go, allow the other person to be and thus, allow you to be.

One can ask a simple question of oneself: why am I to be the judge? When choosing to be a judge, you already position yourself in a lonely place, one that will never inform you of how much you really lose in life.

Shell off the judge's robe and become a loving and compassionate Human-Being. The road leading to your destination will then become an easier path to walk on.

Fear and judgement are alike, sometimes even stemming from the same origins, creating the same results, and so let go of fears as well.

Understand, the majority of your fears are not only composed of things that you went through in life, but actually originate from your environment, society and history.

True courage is the willingness to take everything as new, exercise wise cautiousness and proceed with unobstructed awareness and alertness toward your destination. Remember to use the *Truth-Resonance-Gong* to aid you on your way.

Next we come to a very delicate balancing act that might require us to be as skilled and patient as a trapeze artist – the setting of boundaries.

In Tai-Chi, as in most marshal arts, the demonstration to what may happen when one is over-stepping one's own boundaries is decisive, swift, and many time painful.

In the same way, in life, we have to recognize what boundaries we should have and where to place them. I hope you have noticed that I used the term 'should have', because so many times there are boundaries that are forced upon us, which we might need to question.

If you compare a Tai-Chi master and a ballet dancer, you will find that they have a couple of major things in common.

Both types of artists alter their centre of gravity, when they lift any one of their legs, so to keep their balance, and prepare for the next move.

They both negotiate where to step next, before they put down their leg, which means they know that the ground they are about to step on is stable.

Both types of artists also know that they must keep an agile condition of their mind and body in order to be able to maintain a surviving standard.

The reason I am illustrating these examples to you is because one cannot help but be in awe when watching these artists demonstrating their crafts.

We all have to perform balancing acts throughout our days. We all have to become experts in doing so, but I can already hear your response, experts?

Well, there is a secret, which allows us to have a shortcut. The secret to living a life of well defined boundaries, without over-extending ourselves to the degree of harming ourselves and others, is to check what base you are based on.

I mentioned previously how important it is to be based in love versus judgement and fear. I would add to it now that it is also important to be based in patience and compassion.

Imagine that what you are about to say or do, is being said or done to you. Will you approve of it? Will it be empowering or disempowering to you?

If you train yourself to do it each and every time prior to acting, you will incorporate a 'slow motion' effect to your actions although, you may become so proficient in it, that you will be able to be very fast indeed in doing so.

What will you gain from it?

Well, countless arguments and/or quarrels will never be born. You will be far more graceful in your being and communications. You will have far better relationships, including with your own conscious – far less guilt, blame, and general waste of time and effort.

If and when you feel angry or agitated, you imagine counting from one to ten, just before you burst forth with your reaction. Your body will actually rebalance itself, lowering your blood pressure, reducing the emergency hormones generation, and will allow you to think again. When you gather your thoughts, the reflection in the mirror lessens its distortion, and suddenly, you can release that which clutched you so tight – release, let go, breathe and re-focus.

Any action demands energy. A person must budget all types of energies, so as to not run short.

This brings me to a very sore point. Many times we will take all the right actions, say the right things, and be very alert and aware of everything in our lives, and yet, we will either fail miserably, or pay dearly, in one way or another.

Using a term from philosophy, we have to check our premise.

How many times people make assumptions, their original premise is based on what they know, understand, comprehend, or experienced, but the premise can be entirely untrue.

For example, there is a saying that love conquers everything, or love can build bridges where none can be built, but no one said 'as long as both parties have willingness to do so.'

Part of setting correct boundaries is also clarifying the meaning of words between people, so when one defines love as one thing, the other person does not reduce the value of it. Similarly, to a currency exchange calculation, you have to denote the value of each in order to be able to exchange them.

In order to have good relationships, whether they last for a moment or a life time, you have to deal with equal values.

Our next aid deals, as well, with some of these issues, and is closely related to the importance of boundaries' setting.

Next, we have to learn how to negotiate our priorities.

Our priorities are usually divided to types according to the realm they cover namely, physical, emotional, survival, living, parenthood and so on.

Needless to say that some of the items cannot, for most part, be delayed, and if they are delayed, the consequences might bring us to dire states. It is here that we must learn to negotiate our priorities, because it is better for us to be responding rather than reacting, behaving proactively, rather than reactively.

A parent has to attend to the baby's needs, because they took on a responsibility that puts the baby in a higher priority than their own needs, but even there, you will find that teaching the baby the basic skills of relationship's give and take, may be helpful.

There are too many examples that one can mention, but we do not want to loose sight of the wood for the trees here. Therefore, let us state the most important point, which is listing your priorities, duties, demands made on you, roles and wishes. Identifying which ones are real, and which you may let go of or delegate. Try and be true to yourself, both in your own regard and in relation to others, there is no space here neither for sacrificing yourself, or being self-centered.

Negotiation of priorities has to be done daily, because life is in a flow, and change demands so. If we want to be flowing with the river of life, we must cease to be rigid and develop flexibility.

There are other types of aids that are also required. It is one thing to remove obstacles, but another in enchanting, encouraging, promoting and enticing.

In the flow of life

I begged to dance freely

I shook all constraints off

And revealed my soul's freedom

At The Gate

Enchanting the soul to being is like the dance of life.

First we have to have understanding; it is very much like recognizing the rhythm in music, so you would know which dance it would be.

Then you have to free yourself, to start moving to the music, and this we have done with the aids mentioned previously, to release us from any restrictions to the movement.

Now it is the time to actually engage in the dance.

Let us go back to our artists, the Tai-Chi master and the ballet dancer. They too have to warm up their muscles, be well rested and fed, have willingness to move, and have their trust in themselves.

Think of enchanting your soul to being as a ritual. Go through your day, duties, obligations and tasks while, in the back of your mind you will hold your soul's light and your destination in a prime position, like a full rich backdrop – the canvas on which you draw the illustration of this day.

It is easier to do so if you hold two points of view at the same time, the observer's vantage point of view, as well as the actual performer.

Although, our soul and body form one singular being in life on Earth, they are actually not homogenic-singular. The body is of the Earth and has a given duration of appearance while, the soul is of the Divine and thus, eternal.

If, while you live your life on Earth, you understand that it has two facets, you will gain a deeper understanding.

Consequently, enchanting the soul to being is actually shifting your focus. If you look at a hurricane, at the edges of it there is a lot of activity, force and even chaos while, as you draw to its centre, it becomes calmer and calmer, until you reach the quite centre that is called 'the eye of the storm'.

The centrifugal movement and force at the edges of the hurricane can be akin to the daily energies that are forcing us to 'do'. It is in our drawing inwardly that we will experience calm, and find unity with our soul.

Where is the gate then?

The gate is within your consciousness. The gate is the mindset that you choose to have when, with reverence, love and appreciation, you approach your soul. When you have the intent to approach your soul, and engage in keeping it within your mind and actions most of your day, you will arrive at the gate, at the necessary mindset.

This gate, like all gates, has a lock. The correct mindset brought you to the gate, and your key to unlock the gate is what you bring to the dance.

You see, to be ready, physically, emotionally and intellectually, is not enough. In order for the person to be able to dance, not only he has to be ready, recognize the rhythm and know which dance will fit this music, but he also has to have something more – the spiritual readiness.

The spiritual readiness is that which elates us, induces the fire of the creative self, and brings forth the streaming waters of our inner fountainhead. The spiritual readiness is a yearning force for greater growth and development, because it recognizes the Divine as its source, and yearns to have communion with it.

This is the key.

This key is delicate, and you might only see glimpses of it on regular basis, but this is what is required.

After unlocking the gate, comes the action of opening it.

The light was shimmering

I was shivering

My excitement was palatable

And I at last - arrived

The Openner

I hope you are not one of those readers, who only read excerpts from books, and jumps between pages and chapters, as all the pages that I have written right from the beginning of this book to this, suppose to help you arrive at that state that will allow you to use the soul's openner effectively.

You must know that like an idiom, you might read it, but it might take you years to comprehend and understand it indeed. Therefore, go back to the beginning of this book, and read every word of it – each and every one of those words is my gift to you.

What then is the soul's openner, and why did I spell it so.

I took a 'poetic license' in spelling the openner with double 'n', as I wanted to accentuate that part of the word, and make a point of differentiating it from a 'can opener'. Please indulge me, and let's continue.

The soul within us may be hidden, but it is always working in our lives, though at times we feel it is dormant. The strife that we go though, most of the times, is evidence to the existence of an inner tear that we carry, between our soul and the person's will.

Let me remind you what I have stated earlier – the soul shines continuously, but we might not be able to see or show it.

The openner has two actions in one. The first action is similar to pushing the gate wings open after unlocking the lock. The second action is the act of walking through it to the other side – crossing the threshold.

The first action will constitute any number of methods to enchant your life, after you unchained yourself from the daily burdens. Now, it is the time to promote yourself, so you may feel like a bird that is ready to soar to the skies of your soul.

There are numerous ways of going about it, and it is what I referred to earlier, as the different types of aids that are the building and encouraging ones. It may be anything from a quite meditation, to a tour at the art galleries of your nearest town. It could be drinking high quality coffee at a side café while, listening to the music and watching the children play, or to walking on the beach when the tide is coming in.

You may choose the methods that are most enchanting to you, but first let us define the word enchanting. Oxford dictionary defines it as: Charm, Delight, bewitch. Therefore, choose the aid which will do that for you, and bring yourself to a place where you would become elated, where an inner excitement will want to bubble out and bring a warm smile to your face, mind and heart. Remember the joy a baby may feel – try to feel it too.

The second action is the one that allows you to walk through the gate, which also asks what it is that you had brought here with you.

That which you bring forth with, is the conglomeration of your vocation, purpose, intent, skills set, talents, and of course, your willingness. Your dreams are made of this stuff; only going through the gate will allow you to mould them to form.

The openner is really the act of giving expression to the soul's creativity. The vehicle of expression, may it be art, writing, bringing up children, or anything else, is becoming the openner-assigned. The definition of the openner-assigned is temporary, as it is the action that constitutes the openner's definition, and you may have multiple fields of openner-assigned.

If you can imagine your soul's dance like '*Spirit Floating Cadence*', what will it be?

Spirit Floating Cadence is the rhythm of the floating pulse of Spirit. In our own body we recognize the pulse as the measure of the blood flow in our system. You know that you can change the tempo, the speed, and force of the pulse, as per your activity, and your response to your experiences.

Spirit, within us, also flows. It, too, has a pulse, and its rhythm is the floating cadence.

When you feel a quickening at the depth of your being, ask where it comes from, and if it is from your soul – pay attention and listen.

This quickening, this *Spirit Floating Cadence* is what you should feel when you are about to walk through the gate. Actually, it will start with a silent excitement as you will be opening the gate's wings, and by the time you will be ready to walk through, it will engulf you utterly, like an immense wave.

When you go forth, and choose the method in which you will express your creativity, this feeling will aid you in recognizing its truthfulness.

We are creatures of The Creator, we are miniature creators ourselves and thus, creativity is our innate and prime state of being. Unlike many who were trained to believe that we are just born in order to work hard and suffer, and then death will come as a great relief, I believe that our existence is far superior and much more beautiful.

I stated that the soul's openner is an action; I would like to say that here too, it is important to understand what action means.

I am reminded of a true story that was told about a great artist. One day, while he was sitting in his garden, a neighbour passed by and asked whether he was resting, the artist replied that oh, no, he was working. On another day, the same neighbour passed by again and saw the artist painting, he remarked, oh, you are working, the artist replied oh, no, I am resting.

This is to illustrate that 'doing', as in action, may come in many forms. The artist needed to look deeply into the play of colours that were created by the light, as the day was advancing, so he will be able to record them then on his canvass, as authentically as possible. Therefore, looking is a form of researching, contemplating, analysing and concluding.

Let your actions be versatile. Let your action take many forms of expression, because it is in the opportunities to express yourself that you open up the flow and allow for your soul to shine through, and you will then witness the *Spirit Floating Cadence*.

In the silence of my heart
A faint movement was evoked
I listened very intently
And found my own cadence

Your Soul Is Shining

You are here. You have witnessed it, if only for a moment. Is it not incredible?

You have seen the Truth, you have experienced it, you know now that your soul shines continuously. How else can you explain the fact that every time you look intently – you can see it then?

I hope I am not prematurely assuming here, that while reading this book, and while practicing some of its recommendations, you have had some special moments.

It is important to acknowledge any glimpse of it, whether it was for a short or a long moment. It is important for us to know that we can do it, that we have not lost it, as we actually cannot lose it, but we might mount so many obstacles on the way, that we might fool ourselves to think that we have lost it.

It will help if you can also allow your attention to acknowledge that sublime part of you, so when you walk you will be able to see yourself as the vessel of light that you are, and walk tall. You will be able to know that you are a conduit, and part of the whole.

Imagine that you are like a walking burning bush, or that you have a constant light-fall, like a water-fall, streaming over and into you.

Your soul is shining continuously, it is you that have to allow it to be seen and witnessed by others, and you will achieve it, as you apply more and more the methods to remove the veils, the obstacles and any falsehood.

In the quite moments, when you allow yourself to calm down and just be, in excitement moments, when you allow joy to fill you up, in moments of emptiness, when all you do is look for the beauty and the nature of things, know that you are one with you soul, know that you are yourself.

Let go of expectations, because you and I have a minute imagination in comparison to The Divine. When you have the courage to open up, you will discover that you do not become vulnerable, rather you become innocent.

Your innocence will reward you with newness. You will see then everything with new eyes, eyes that are not bogged down with preconceived ideas and notions.

When you allow your soul to shine right through you, all your actions, words, and behaviours will be special, as they will come from your authentic self. Your true nature and greatness will have the opportunity to lead you to true happiness.

While being comfortable in tangible riches, it is the intangible that allows you to live life to the full.

The prophet Jeremiah spoke of it in an allegory as follows:

"For he shall be as a tree planted by the waters, and that spreadeth out her roots by the river, and shall not see when heat cometh, but her leaf shall be green; and shall not be careful in the year of drought, neither shall cease from yielding fruit." (Jeremiah 17/8)

An inner and constant riches on every level of our being is possible, when we are connected. The waters are The Divine streaming throughout the whole of Creation and all its parts.

We have to know that we are connected, we

have to let go of the belief that we are separated.

Only then we truly shine – effortlessly.

The Seed of My Soul

Right there at my centre
Lies the seed of my soul
Where once was put to sprout
Grow, shine and be

But other forces wished it stopped
And the seed shrivelled and heed
No light, no love, no comfort
Lay there dormant and thin

One day I woke up to see it
Shrunk, and all darkness around it
And I leaned to blow life into it
Wishing the light will shine it live

How life can be brought to dormant
How light can shoo the darkness
How the growth of an healthy seed
Can occupy its original size

And awoken it will be
To the beauty of life
To God's grace
And to breathe.

Maintaining The Openness

In this instant, the word openness does not denote an open state that allows other things to get in, but rather a wholeness that allows the flow of Spirit. Like a solid pipe of gold, free of leaks.

In order for Spirit to flow through us, we must be open to the Light, because it is the life force. When we are filled with Light, our soul can express itself and while it does so, Spirit flows through us.

If you ever looked at a candle, I am sure that you have seen that the whole length of the wick is covered with wax, and as long as the candle flame was not distinguished unnaturally, it would burn right to the end.

We are like the candle, and more. Our wax

is endless, like Jeremiah's waters; we are capable to shine our light from the moment of our birth, to our death and beyond.

Therefore, it is up to us to maintain our openness. It is up to us to do all that I spoke of and remember that we are called to it.

Have faith and hope, have joy and work, have yourself and your soul, so you may go forth, so you may flow.

Your flow may take many forms of expression, and that is good. Let it be.

Remember that life does not ask of you to struggle, but it does ask of you to fulfill your vocation – to fulfill the purpose that called for your birth.

I made a point of writing all of this in a format of a pocket book, so you can refer to it continually, and it will be fast and easy for you to do so.

This is the end of the book – and the beginning of a good life.

Be Strong and of Good Courage!

www.ingramcontent.com/pod-product-compliance
Lightning Source LLC
Chambersburg PA
CBHW031637160426
43196CB000006B/448